Ms. Frizzle's Adventures
MEDIEVAL CASTLE

Ms. Frizzle's Adventures
MEDIEVAL CASTLE

by **JOANNA COLE**
illustrated by **BRUCE DEGEN**

ARMOR *by* ARNOLD

12th CENTURY
CHAIN MAIL ARMOR
SMALL LINKS OF
METAL ALL JOINED
TOGETHER

14th CENTURY
PLATE ARMOR
MADE OF SOLID
METAL PIECES

Welcome to Ms. Frizzle's Class

TODAY IS FRIDAY 13

SCHOLASTIC PRESS
new york

Library of Congress Cataloging-in-Publication Data • Cole, Joanna. Ms. Frizzle's
adventures: medieval castle / by Joanna Cole; illustrated by Bruce Degen.
p. cm. • Summary: When Ms. Frizzle and her student Arnold follow an underground
passage beneath Craig's Castle Shop and find themselves in the middle of a
siege of a 12th century English castle, they learn a great deal about both castles
and the Middle Ages. 1. Castles--Juvenile literature. 2. Civilization, Medieval—Juvenile
literature. [1. Castles. 2. Civilization, Medieval. 3. England--Civilization—1066-1485.]
I. Degen, Bruce, ill. II. Title. GT3550 .C65 2002 728.8'1— dc21 2002005257
ISBN 0-590-10820-4 (hardcover) — 10 9 8 7 6 5 4 3 2 1   03 04 05 06 07   Printed
in Mexico   49 • First edition, August 2003. • The text type was set in GillSans. • The
illustrator used pen and ink, watercolor, color pencil, and gouache for the paintings in
this book. • The author thanks Carol Hart and her children, Jamieson, Rose,
and Phoebe, for giving her the idea to write about castles. The author
and illustrator would like to thank Nancy Wu of The Cloisters
Museum and The Metropolitan Museum of Art
for her careful review of the manuscript
and illustrations.

For Sir Cooper Garff
—J.C.

For Janet Carlile,
whose friendship and love
have withstood the siege of time
in the Castle Keep of our hearts
—B.D.

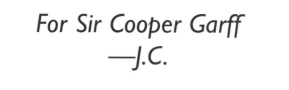

It was a bright Saturday morning,
and I, Ms. Frizzle, was on the move!
I had just taken out a book from the library
when I saw someone I knew.
It was Arnold – one of my favorite students!
He was on his way into Craig's Castle Shop.

WALKERVILLE PUBLIC LIBRARY

WALKERVILLE TOWN HALL

From Ms. Frizzle's Castle Book...

WHAT IS A CASTLE?

A castle is a fortified home where a king or nobleman once lived with his family and his army of soldiers.

GREAT TOWER WHERE THE FAMILY LIVED

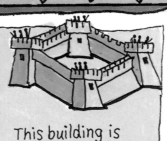

This building is fortified, and it has soldiers. But no family lives here. So it is not a castle. It is a fort.

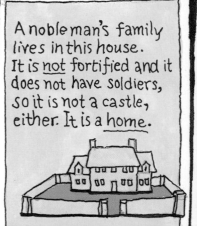

A nobleman's family lives in this house. It is not fortified and it does not have soldiers, so it is not a castle, either. It is a home.

What a coincidence!
My library book was about castles.
I knew Arnold would be interested in my book, so I followed him inside the shop.

Craig's Castle Shop

ADD A MOAT TO YOUR CASTLE! ½ PRICE

HOW TO FORTIFY YOUR HOME

1. Build it out of stone instead of wood.
2. Make the walls very thick.
   Wall is made of stones outside and filled with rubble inside.

3. Put a stone wall around it.
4. Dig a ditch around the wall.
5. Fill it with water. Now it is called a moat.
6. Make openings for soldiers to shoot from.

AFRICAN CASTLE

MIDDLE EASTERN CASTLE

SPANISH CASTLE

JAPANESE CASTLE

CRAIG, MEET MS. FRIZZLE.

NOT MY TEACHER! IT'S SATURDAY!

HELLO, MS. DRESS...OOPS! I MEAN, MS. FRIZZLE.

Everywhere in the shop there were models of castles from all over the world. And there were shelves and shelves of figurines. Craig, the shop owner, was showing Arnold a collection of people for an English castle. Arnold and Craig both gave me a warm welcome!

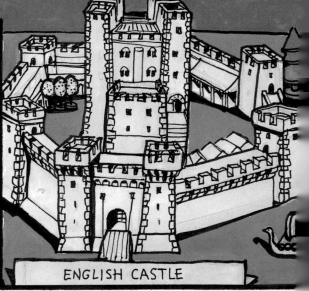

ENGLISH CASTLE

I couldn't help noticing
a handle on the floor.
Since I, Ms. Frizzle,
am naturally curious,
I experimented by pulling on it.
It was a trapdoor to the basement.
Arnold is always so adventurous!
He insisted on going down.
Naturally, I followed him,
and Craig came down to join us.

INDIAN CASTLE

WELSH CASTLE

SCOTTISH CASTLE

What a surprise!
There was a sewing studio in the basement.
A talented clothing designer named Crystal
was making medieval costumes.
Arnold wanted to try on a squire's outfit.
I try to encourage my students,
so I got into a costume, too.

THIS CHAIN MAIL FITS JUST RIGHT!

HOW IS YOUR COSTUME, ARNOLD?

MMMRRMFF...

THE COSTUMES ARE NOT FOR SALE. THEY'RE FOR OUR MEDIEVAL FESTIVAL.

THIS IS FUN. I HARDLY EVER GET VISITORS.

TRY ON THIS WORD!

MEDIEVAL

MORE ANCIENT

MEDIEVAL

comes from a word that means "MIDDLE AGES"

MIDDLE

Medieval times came in the middle —between ancient times and the more modern world.

MORE MODERN

When Arnold found a mysterious tunnel lit by flaming torches, I went along. Craig and Crystal did, too.

Arnold wanted to see where the passage
went, so he ran faster and faster.
I, Ms. Frizzle, kept up the pace,
and Craig and Crystal followed us eagerly.
Finally, we saw light at the end of
the tunnel.

COME BACK!

YOU FORGOT YOUR SHIELD, MA'AM.

HELP!

WHEN WERE CASTLES BUILT?

The first castles were constructed over 1,000 years ago.

The last ones were built around 600 years ago.

The first castles were simple.

They became more elaborate as time went by.

WHAT WERE CASTLES FOR?

A castle was the center of life for a whole community. Sometimes, but not always, a town grew up around a castle.

Suddenly, trumpets blared.
The lord of the castle was riding out of the gate
with his army thundering behind him.
Everyone stopped working to wave and cheer.
Tom said that Lord Robert and his men
were going to help fight a war for the king.

THE LORD FIGHTS FOR THE KING.

AND WE KNIGHTS FIGHT FOR THE LORD.

SPEAKING OF KNIGHTS, I HAVE HUNDREDS OF THEM IN MY SHOP.

YOU MUST BE A VERY POWERFUL LORD!

Fighters

Lord Robert
owns the castle and its lands

Knights
sworn to fight for Lord Robert

Men at Arms
foot soldiers employed by Lord Robert

Squires
Knights' helpers

Peg explained that while the lord was away,
Lady Anne was in charge of the castle.
I knew Arnold wanted to help her,
so I led everyone up to the tower
where the lady was looking out over the land.

THIS IS **SO** EXCITING! THANKS FOR BRINGING US ON THIS ADVENTURE, ARNOLD!

NO PROBLEM, CRYSTAL. ADVENTURE IS ARNOLD'S MIDDLE NAME!

NO, IT ISN'T. IT'S MATTHEW.

WHO'S WHO AT THE CASTLE?

Lady Anne
Wife of Lord Robert. She supervises the servants and makes sure everything inside the castle runs smoothly.
   When her husband is away, she is responsible for the protection of the castle, too.

Constable Peter
commander of the garrison

The Garrison
the guards and soldiers who are always there to defend the castle

From the castle top, we could see for miles. Suddenly, hoofbeats sounded in the distance. A soldier yelled, "It's Baron Griffin and his army! He is going to try to capture the castle!"

BARON GRIFFIN AND LORD ROBERT HAVE BEEN ENEMIES FOR A LONG TIME.

EACH ONE WANTS THE OTHER'S LAND AND CASTLE...

NOW THE BARON HAS FINALLY MADE HIS MOVE!

WHO'S <u>NOT</u> IN THE CASTLE?
Baron Griffin

WHAT WERE CASTLES FOR?

A castle was the command post used to control the lord's land.

FROM THE CASTLE WE CAN SEE...

IF WORKERS IN THE FIELDS ARE DOING THEIR JOBS...

IF POACHERS ARE HUNTING IN LORD ROBERT'S FORESTS...

IF ANYONE COMES ONTO LORD ROBERT'S ESTATE.

FROM THE CASTLE WE CAN SEND OUT SOLDIERS TO HANDLE PROBLEMS.

We looked out over the fields.
Peasants were hurrying away from
the approaching army.
As they ran, they loaded crops into carts
and drove cows and sheep toward the castle.

DON'T LEAVE ANYTHING FOR THE ENEMY TO EAT!

WE CAN'T CARRY ANY MORE!

THEN SET IT ON FIRE!

JUST HURRY!

WHO'S WHO AROUND THE CASTLE?

PEASANTS

Peasants are farmers.
Each peasant family farms
a plot of the castle's land.
Peasants' lives are almost
nothing but work, work, work.

WE GROW FOOD, BUT WE HAVE TO GIVE ALMOST ALL OF IT TO THE LORD...

SO WE ARE OFTEN HUNGRY.

Lady Anne went to her private chamber and called in the constable and her adviser, Sir Gilbert. I always give good advice, so I went along to help plan the strategy to defend the castle.
Quickly, Lady Anne wrote a letter to Lord Robert.

THE SOLDIERS MUST SHOOT ARROWS FROM THE TOP OF THE CASTLE, MY LADY.

QUITE RIGHT, STRANGE KNIGHT.

CONSTABLE PETER, GIVE THE ORDER!

AT ONCE, MY LADY.

W HO'S WHO IN THE CASTLE?

SIR GILBERT
Lord Robert's uncle who lives in the castle

LADIES-IN-WAITING
companions and helpers to Lady Anne

The attacking army had come closer.
Our garrison shot arrows at them.
But some of the soldiers hid in siege towers —
wooden towers on wheels.
Other soldiers pushed the towers
close to the castle.

OH, NO!

THE ARROWS WON'T GO THROUGH THE WOOD!

WET ANIMAL HIDES PROTECT TOWERS FROM FLAMING ARROWS

ENEMY FILLS MOAT IN WITH DIRT AND ROCKS

MOAT

DESIGNED FOR DEFENSE

EARLY DESIGN: CRENELLATIONS

In peacetime, lookouts use large openings.

In war, archers use the same openings.

PROBLEM: Archers can get hit easily by enemy arrows.

IMPROVED DESIGN: SPECIAL OPENINGS CALLED ARROW SLITS FOR ARCHERS

On the outside, a narrow slit keeps most arrows out.

On the inside, space is wide enough for the archer's body.

RESULT: Fewer archers get hit.

The army was using the towers to get into our castle.
From behind the battlements of the castle,
our small garrison could fight off a huge army.
But if the army got inside, the castle guards
would be outnumbered.
They wouldn't have a chance in hand-to-hand combat.
I, Ms. Frizzle, knew one thing for sure —
we *had* to keep the baron's troops *out*!

But the battle was just beginning.
As summer turned to fall,
the siege dragged on and on.
My castle book said that some sieges
lasted for six months.
I hoped that wouldn't happen to us!

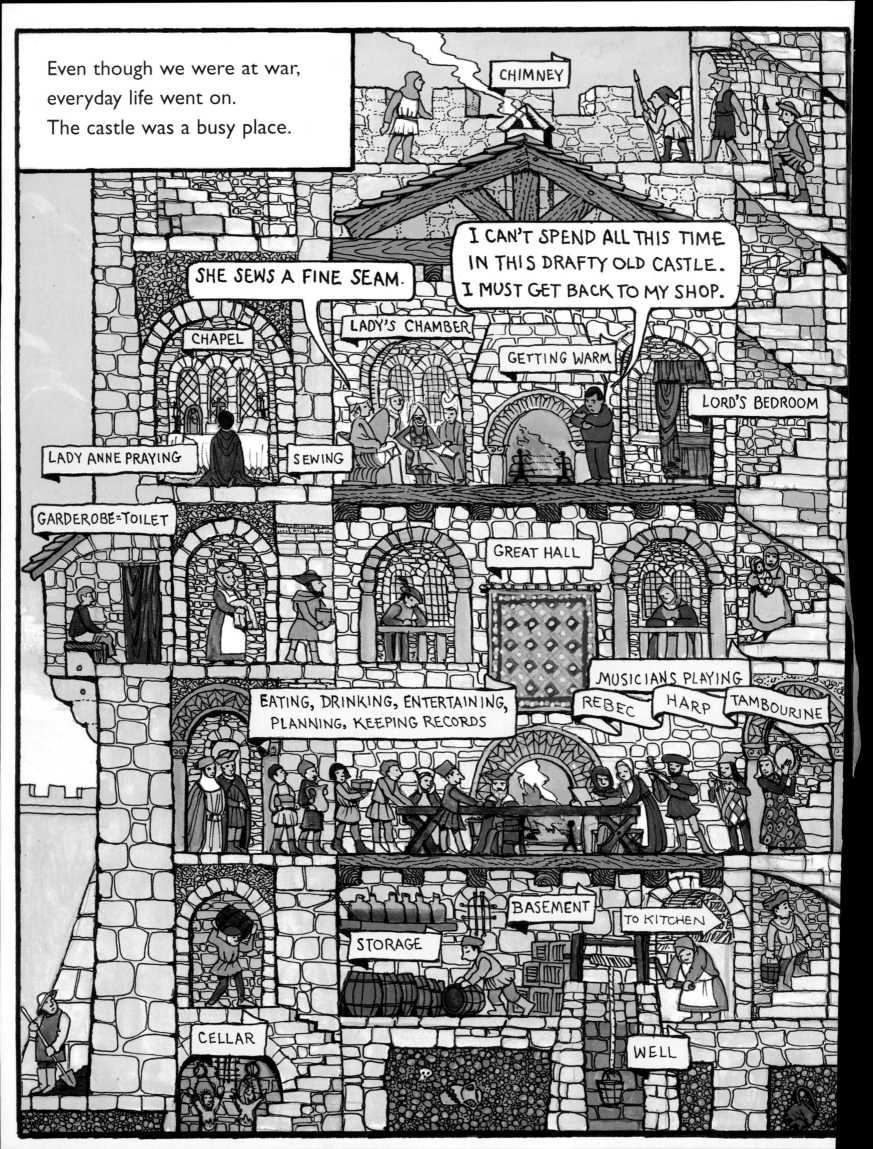

Even though we were at war, everyday life went on. The castle was a busy place.

Luckily, we had plenty of water.
It came from a well under the castle.
Our food was running low.
The besieging army was hungry, too.
But the baron would not give up.
The siege wasn't over yet!

Now Baron Griffin gave a new order.
He told his soldiers to a dig a tunnel
right up to the castle.
Since the Baron's men were underground,
our lookouts couldn't see them.

I'M ALMOST THERE... I HOPE.

The enemy soldiers began digging a hole under the castle. As the men enlarged the space, they used wooden posts to prop up the heavy stone.

When the space was large enough, the diggers made a fire to burn up the posts.

The posts crumbled into ashes, and the stone wall fell down.

Lord Robert's army drove off the baron and his men. The garrison easily captured the few enemy soldiers who had gotten inside the castle.
Joyfully, we all welcomed the returning army.

RETREAT!!

WE LIVE TO FIGHT ANOTHER DAY.

THANK GOODNESS!

WHY DID PEOPLE STOP BUILDING CASTLES?

About 600 years ago, armies started using gunpowder to shoot cannonballs.

This new power made it easy to break stone walls.

As a defense, castles just didn't work anymore.

Lord Robert called for a celebration.
There was hardly any food left in the castle,
but the army had brought back new supplies.
The castle people feasted with gusto —
they'd been hungry for such a long time.

THE GREAT HALL
Lords, ladies, clergy, and guests feasted here.

THE HIGH TABLE

Hollowed-out slabs of bread served as plates.

CENTER TABLE

WHAT THEY ATE
1. Roast Swan and...
2. Pheasant presented with feathers on
3. Rich stews of meat, vegetables, and spices served on bread
4. Grilled fish
5. Dried fruits and nuts
6. Pigeons baked in fancy pastry
7. Wine, ale~only rich people had glasses. Others drank from leather tankards or wooden goblets.

As for me, I went home to relax.
It had been such an exciting Saturday.
Who knew what might happen on Sunday?
I, Ms. Frizzle, would be ready for anything!

DON'T BELIEVE EVERYTHING YOU READ!

(Especially in this book)

Some things are just pretend, and others need a little explanation.

- At least one thing in this book is just pretend. A wristwatch cannot take you back in time — no matter how fancy it is. (Not even if it tells the date, reads your e-mail, and knows how old your sister is.)

- In this book, it may seem as if the people besieging the castle are bad and the ones inside the castle are good. However, they are all probably just about the same. For all we know, Lord Robert might attack Baron Griffin's castle some day.

- The people in this book all talk to each other easily. But in medieval England, people spoke an old kind of English. It would have been hard for Ms. Frizzle's group and the castle dwellers to understand each other.

- You might not have liked life in a castle. It was cold, smelly, and uncomfortable. People did not take baths very often, and they usually had fleas. Only the nobles had beds; others slept on the floor. Also, there was no TV in those days.

- One thing is true that may seem false. People sometimes think that women had no power in the olden days. But the lady of the castle really was the boss when the lord went away.

- It is also true that Arnold was brave. We're so proud of him.

- And Ms. Frizzle really did wear a knight's armor. You know how she loves dressing up!